WHAT IS
CITIZENSHIP?

Jessica Pegis

🌳 Crabtree Publishing Company
www.crabtreebooks.com

W9-BMF-407

CITIZENSHIP IN ACTION

Author: Jessica Pegis

Series research and development: Reagan Miller

Editors: Petrice Custance and Reagan Miller

Proofreader: Janine Deschenes

Design and photo research: Margaret Amy Salter

Prepress technician: Margaret Amy Salter

Print and production coordinator: Katherine Berti

Photographs

Shutterstock.com: rmnoa357: page 7; Ververidis Vasilis: page 10; arindambanerjee: page 16 (bottom); Drop of Light: page 17 (top right)

All other images from Shutterstock

Library and Archives Canada Cataloguing in Publication

Pegis, Jessica, author
      What is citizenship? / Jessica Pegis.

(Citizenship in action)
Includes index.
Issued in print and electronic formats.
ISBN 978-0-7787-2596-1 (hardback).--
ISBN 978-0-7787-2602-9 (paperback).--
ISBN 978-1-4271-1773-1 (html)

      1. Citizenship--Juvenile literature. 2. Civics--Juvenile literature.
I. Title.

JF801.P44 2016   j323.6   C2016-904138-7
                                      C2016-904139-5

Library of Congress Cataloging-in-Publication Data

CIP available at the Library of Congress

Crabtree Publishing Company

www.crabtreebooks.com   1-800-387-7650

Printed in Canada/082016/TL20160715

Published in Canada
Crabtree Publishing
616 Welland Ave.
St. Catharines, Ontario
L2M 5V6

Published in the United States
Crabtree Publishing
PMB 59051
350 Fifth Avenue, 59th Floor
New York, New York 10118

Published in the United Kingdom
Crabtree Publishing
Maritime House
Basin Road North, Hove
BN41 1WR

Published in Australia
Crabtree Publishing
3 Charles Street
Coburg North
VIC 3058

What is in this book?

What is citizenship?

Citizenship means being part of a **community**. A community is a place where people live, work, and play. Being a **citizen** is like being part of a family. Your family meets your needs by making sure you have enough food to eat. Your community meets your needs by fixing roads and building new schools.

A citizen's community can be small, such as a school, or big, such as a country. Citizens usually belong to just one country. They feel a special pride for their country.

Citizens also care about people in other countries. They want the world to be a good and safe place for everyone.

What makes a citizen?

Some citizens are born in their community. Other people become citizens when they move to a new community.

When you are born, you become a citizen of the country you are born in.

If you move to another country, you can **apply** to be a citizen. You must obey all the rules of the new country. You must also pass a test to prove you know some facts about the new country.

New citizens feel pride in their country, just like citizens who were born there.

Be an active citizen

Active citizens play an important role in their community. If they spot a problem they try to fix it. If there are people in their community who are in need, active citizens work together to help them.

THANK YOU

Active citizens work hard to make their community a great place for everyone.

What are some ways you could be an active citizen in your community?

Rights of citizenship

Citizenship gives each person **rights**. A right is something you are allowed to have or do. Your rights are protected by **laws**. A law is a rule made by **government** and is **enforced** by police officers.

Active citizens speak up for their rights and also for the rights of others.

All citizens have the right to:

- ☑ Be treated fairly
- ☑ **Vote** for their leaders
- ☑ Follow their faith
- ☑ Speak out and share ideas
- ☑ Choose where to live

Responsibilities of citizenship

Citizens have a **responsibility** to make their community a great place for everyone. A responsibility is something you should take care of or do. Active citizens work hard to be responsible in their community.

All citizens have the responsibility to:

- Obey the laws
- Treat others fairly
- Speak out about unfairness
- Get involved with their community
- **Respect** the environment

Rights and Responsibilities

Active citizens know that rights and responsibilities go together.

Citizens have rights. Citizens also have the responsibility to protect the rights of others. Even if a citizen has the right to do something, the citizen still has the responsibility to protect the rights of others.

Active citizens know that their actions affect others.

What do you think?

Sofia and Todd decided it would be fun to yell "Earthquake!" in the school cafeteria.

They knew there was no earthquake, but many students did not. They ducked under the lunch tables. They were afraid. The teachers tried to find out what was going on.

They were worried about the students' safety. Sofia and Todd thought it was a good prank. Do you think Sofia and Todd had the right to play the prank? Were Sofia and Todd protecting the rights of others during the prank? Why or why not?

What is government?

Countries meet the needs of citizens through government. A government is a group of people who run a country, province, state, or community.

Citizens **elect** leaders by voting for them. Citizens have a say in how the government is run.

Who are some people in government?

A president or prime minister is an important person in government. He or she leads the whole country. He or she works with other people in government who pass laws and help run the country.

Police, firefighters, teachers, and many other workers are also part of the government. They help to provide the services that citizens need.

Government and citizens

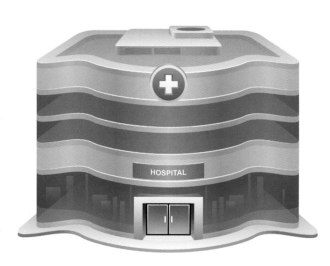

How does a community stay strong?

Communities stay strong by making sure every citizen's needs are met. Government provides some of the services to meet a citizen's needs.

A government can build schools and hospitals. It can supply clean water and pick up garbage. It can run buses and trains. It can make laws to keep citizens safe.

What do you think?

Sleepyville is going to sleep. The workers are tired. The fire fighters will no longer put out fires. The bus drivers will no longer drive the buses. The police will no longer fight crime.

The citizens of Sleepyville are not worried. They are sure no one will notice.

What could happen to Sleepyville? What advice would you give the workers and citizens of Sleepyville?

Sleepyville

Working together

Active citizens work together to make their community a great place for everyone. They make sure their neighborhoods are

safe and friendly places. They avoid littering. They volunteer at school or at the library. They help neighbors by cutting grass or shoveling snow. They report any dangers to the police.

What are some ways that you can be an active citizen in your own community?

What do you think?

Every day on his way to school, Kamal passes the club house in the local park. It is covered in ugly graffiti. There is litter on the ground and on the steps. Nobody seems to care how bad it looks. Kamal would like to do something, but he is only one person. He wonders what he could do. What advice do you have for Kamal?

Learning more

Books

Dalrymple, Lisa. *Be the Change in the World.* Crabtree Publishing, 2015.

Hanson, Anders. *Do Something for Others: The Kids' Book of Citizenship.* Super Sandcastle, 2014.

Web Sites

Learn all about citizenship here:
http://www.congressforkids.net/citizenship_intro.htm

Find out about the Canadian Civil Liberties Association here:
https://ccla.org/education/elementary/learning-tools/

Check out this site for some cool facts about civics:
http://constitutioncenter.org/learn/educational-resources/we-the-civics-kids/

Have some fun and take part in The Democracy Project:
http://pbskids.org/democracy/parents-and-teachers/vote/citizenship-city/

Words to Know

apply (uh-PLAHY) verb To request or ask

citizen (SIT-i-sen) noun A person who belongs to a community

community (CU-mu-ni-tee) noun A place where people live, work, and play

elect [ih-lekt] verb To choose a government leader or member by voting for him or her

enforce (en-FAWRS) verb To make sure a rule or law is followed

government [GUHV-ern-muhnt] noun A group of people that run a country, province, state, or community

laws (LAWZ) noun Rules made by government that people must follow

respect (re-SPECKED) noun To follow rules and laws to show you value the rights of others

responsibility (re-SPONS-i-bill-i-tee) noun Something you should take care of or do

right (RITE) noun Something you are allowed to have or do

vote (VOHT) verb Make a choice by marking a ballot or some other method such as raising your hand

A noun is a person, place, or thing.

A verb is an action word that tells you what someone or something does.

Index

About the author

Jessica Pegis is a writer and editor living in Toronto. She has written several books for teens and children in the areas of science, citizenship, and media awareness.